The PLAYER The PREACHER & The PONK

But God...

RUTEZ MASON

Authentic Endeavors Publishing/Kingdom Book Endeavors
Scranton PA

The Player, The Preacher, The Ponk,
But God...
ISBN: 978-1-967041-36-7 (Paperback)
ISBN: 978-1-967041-37-4 (Ebook)
LCCN: 2025918329

KINGDOM
BOOK ENDEAVORS

Dedication

F irst and always—Father, I THANK YOU for grace undeserved, strength unimagined, and love unfailing. You carried me through every valley and lifted me to every mountaintop. This book is a testimony of Your goodness.

To my three sons, Frederick (Pooh Bear), Destin, and Elijah, you are the reason I fought. Your pure, innocent love gave me the courage to rise, to push through pain, and to build a life worthy of you. You are my heartbeat.

To my only granddaughter, Markenzi, my mini-me, my joy, my second wind, you gave me new life and reminded me that legacy is love. You are my sunshine.

To my bonus son, Tywon, I love you deeply. You are family by choice and by heart.

To my amazing husband, Bradford LeVeige, THANK YOU for it all. For standing beside me, believing in me, and loving me through it all.

To my godsons, Rodd Winn and Joseph Green, Nanny loves you. You are cherished beyond measure.

And last, but never least. I dedicate this book to myself. To the woman who endured, who grew, who rose. To the warrior, the nurturer, the visionary. To the one who never gave up. I honor my own journey, my own healing, and my own becoming. This is more than a book. It's a declaration: But GOD...

Table of Contents

Acknowledgments

To my publisher, Teresa Velardi. You have truly been an angel. Thank you for believing in me, for pushing me beyond my limits, and for going far beyond the call of duty. Your heart and dedication have made this book possible.

To Apostle Sandra West Williams, your mentoring and prayers have been a lifeline. Thank you for pouring into me with wisdom and grace.

To my mother, Annie Mae, thank you for praying for me. There is nothing like a praying mother, and your intercession has carried me through storms I never thought I'd survive.

To Tomacenia Hill, your expertise and knowledge were invaluable. Thank you for sharing your brilliance and continuing to work along with me.

To Shaitassia Tyler, I love you, my sweet girl. You're the best, and your love has been a light in my life.

To Kenjel DeSalle, thank you for standing with me. Auntie Tez loves you deeply, and your support has meant the world.

To my girl Chareen Hurst and Renell Davis (My Luke), thank you for your unwavering love and support. You've held me up when I needed it most, and I'm forever grateful.

To my big brother, Elder Melvin Davis, my church buddy and prayer warrior. Thank you for keeping me lifted in prayer and walking beside me in faith. Love always.

And to every soul who stood in the gap, whispered a prayer, or offered a word of encouragement, this book carries your fingerprints. Through it all, I stand not by strength alone, but by grace. Not by chance, but by divine design. Not by me...but GOD.

Testimonies

I just finished reading Rutez Mason's book. It was excellent, well-written, and a great testimony of God's love and grace.

Maxine Jackson

I read this book from cover to cover. It was a good read. I cried, laughed, and rejoiced! God is Faithful.

Mother Lafrance

Chapter One
Daddy's Little Girl

Ruffic's heart swelled with joy when he learned that his wife, Annie Mae, was expecting. The thought of becoming a father again brought an excitement he hadn't felt in years.

Months passed, and when his daughter finally arrived, she entered the world in a way that mirrored her strength—kicking her way into life, feet first. But her arrival came with challenges. One of her tiny legs was broken, and Dr. Cracco's grim warning echoed through the room: One false move, and she will become crippled for the rest of her life. Yet, Ruffic and Annie refused to accept defeat.

They nurtured their baby's leg with unwavering devotion, believing that with love and care, healing was possible. And then, divinely touched—God healed her.

For Ruffic, his daughter was everything. From the moment he held her, he knew he had to do everything for her—even down to choosing her name. With immense pride, he took the first two letters of his name, RU, and added TEZ—naming me RuTez, a name that carried his legacy and love.

I was, am, and always will be
Daddy's little girl.

I grew up under the unwavering protection of my father. He shielded and guarded me, ensuring no harm ever came my way. His love was relentless, an armor that surrounded me against the world's uncertainties. He taught me about life in ways that only a man who had seen the world's darkest corners could—having served as a soldier in the Korean War. To him, the world was tough, unpredictable, and unforgiving, but in his arms, I was safe.

Though he was 45 when I was born—older than most fathers of young children—his love was as youthful as any new dad's excitement. He carried me to school and walked with me hand in hand, ignoring the murmurs from classmates who assumed he was my grandfather. He didn't care. I was his daughter, his pride, his joy.

As I grew, he fought against time, refusing to let his little girl grow up too fast. When the world said it was time for me to mature, he clung to innocence—rocking me to sleep even when I was no longer small, washing out my bottle every morning and refilling it with milk at night, allowing me the comfort of childhood just a little longer. He knew the world I would step into one day and wanted me to feel safe for as long as possible.

Then, at just ten years old, my world shifted. The man who had been my shield, my guide, my everything—was gone. The loss was immeasurable. He had loved me in the way a father should, but he had also cherished me beyond measure. The lessons he had imparted remained, his presence lingering in the memories of his unwavering protection, tenderness, and wisdom. Though he was gone, his love never faded.

In every whispered memory, story shared, and moment of warmth, his love remained a constant force, a guiding light, for I would always be Daddy's little girl.

Chapter Two
What Now?

After my daddy died, the world shifted beneath my feet. Nothing felt steady anymore. The warmth of his protection and the comfort of his voice vanished with him.

My mom worked a lot. She kept a roof over our heads. That meant we didn't get much time together, and our relationship grew strained. I wanted her attention, her care, but I rarely knew how or if it was okay to ask.

Daddy had been my rescuer. My safe place. And when he left, so did my shield.

My grandmother lived with us. She took care of me and my seven siblings while my mother worked. She was stern, no-nonsense, and ran a tight ship. But she never let us go without. There was always a meal on the table, clothes washed and ready. Her kind of love wasn't soft-spoken or gentle, but it held us steady when everything else felt uncertain.

Still, some things hurt deeper than anyone could see. I'd hear things like, "Mason is dead. What are you going to do now?" And sometimes, after a disagreement, certain siblings would throw the words at me, "That's why your daddy is dead." They knew how much he meant to me. They knew how that would cut. And it did.

I cried quietly and frequently, but I didn't expect anyone to notice. I just kept it moving. I didn't have anyone to come to my defense. I was a lonely yet inquisitive little girl left behind in a world full of questions and shadows.

But even in that darkness, there was something else. A still, small voice. Gentle, yet steady. Sometimes, it would speak to me when everything felt too heavy: "You're going to be okay." I never told a soul about that voice. Who would understand?

But now I know it was God. He saw me, even when I felt invisible. And He stayed, when no one else did.

No one ever asked me how I felt after Daddy died. But that didn't stop me from surviving. Or from hoping.

Chapter Three
First Love

I met him when he was standing outside by the pool at my mother's best friend's apartment. I was fourteen. He was seventeen. There was nothing magical about the moment, no love song playing in the background, no dramatic stares across a crowded room. He was trying to show the gang how to rap to a lady, but something about him made me pause. Maybe it was the way he looked me in the eyes. Perhaps it was because I felt noticed.

We exchanged numbers and talked a little. But I didn't pursue anything. Not at first.

I wasn't looking for love. I was looking for peace. My world at home still felt unsettled. My daddy was gone. My mom was busy, firm, and strict. I craved connection. So, one day, I looked him up again. Not because I was in love, but because I needed a friend.

From there, we built something that looked like friendship but felt like a refuge. He became my listening ear, the one person who didn't brush my feelings aside. We'd talk for hours about everything and nothing. Then I started sneaking to see him.

It felt wrong, but it felt right, too. Like the very thing I was missing had found me, he gave me attention and never made me feel small. And when my mom found out I had a boyfriend, she wasn't having it.

She disapproved—and not quietly. Our relationship, already tense, grew more strained. I couldn't understand why she was trying to take away the one thing that made me feel wanted.

As punishment, she started buying things for my baby sister while skipping over me. No new clothes. No little tokens of love. Just silence and cold shoulders. But I'd tell him everything.

He'd always say, "Don't worry about it. I got you." And he did. Whatever my mom bought for my sister, he'd find and buy for me, too—

matching down to the color and size. I wouldn't tell her where I got them from until one day, I slipped.

She came home and saw me wearing a pair of boots.

"Didn't I tell you not to wear your sister's clothes?"

I stood straight. "These are mine."

She then says to me, "Where did you get them?"

I told her the truth: "He bought them for me."

She was stunned. And from then on, he became my quiet provider—the one who filled in the emotional blanks. Our late-night talks drifted from stories to secrets, and our words started leaning closer, like hearts whispering across the line.

I started feeling something. Something warm and unfamiliar. Butterflies. Could I be catching feelings?

Chapter 4
Virginity, Vision,
and the Voice

We didn't have cell phones back then, just landlines. We used to talk on the phone every night for hours, sometimes even falling asleep mid-conversation. We shared everything. As the phone calls grew longer, so did our feelings.

I had this older guy who was crazy about me. He knew what love felt like. He had already been in a relationship before, and he had a toddler. But for me, this was all brand new. I'd never been in a relationship, never been in love. I didn't even know what love was supposed to feel like. All I knew was that it felt good. And I wanted to see where it would lead.

As time went on, we wanted more than late-night phone calls. We wanted to be together in person. But my mom would never allow it.

Not a boyfriend, and definitely not one three years older. She was rooted and grounded in the things of God, and boys weren't part of the plan this early in life. I was a virgin—good, clean, and wholesome as she would say, and her vision for me was clear: save myself for marriage. But the feelings I'd awakened stirred a curiosity I couldn't ignore. My mother wanted to see this boy who was calling her home for me. He came over, and she was not impressed. He was well-groomed, but something about him. She still didn't approve.

So, I started cutting school to see him but maintained my grades so she wouldn't notice. She never checked attendance. His mother wasn't strict. She let me stay at their house during the day, no questions asked. I'd spend the whole day there and still make it home by my normal time. My mother never noticed. At first, the visits were just conversations and some kissing. I didn't know what I was doing, but I learned quickly.

Over time, the lines blurred, the boundaries faded. Then, one day, a year later, it happened. My virginity was broken.

And right there in that moment, I heard it: the voice that had always been with me. A whisper, clear as day. You're not supposed to be doing this. Was I tripping? Was I imagining things? I don't know. But I was too far gone to turn back. I didn't realize then that the voice was trying to protect me—from the long road I was about to walk because of this one decision.

Oh no. I missed my period. I told him. He was so supportive. We met up and went to a planned pregnancy facility to get tested. My heart was pounding as I took the cup into the restroom.

A few moments later, the lady stepped out and said, "It's positive. You're pregnant."

He was happy. I was scared, carrying a mix of emotions, and knowing what had to come next: I had to tell my mother.

He hugged me tightly, asking if I wanted something to eat, just making sure I was good—like he always had. Always present. Always showing up.

I remember my mom being on the phone when I walked in. I didn't say a word. I simply handed her the form that the lady at Planned Parenthood had given me. She looked at it...then looked at me. She was furious.

"He's not going to stay," she said flatly. "He got what he wanted."

I told him exactly what she said. He looked me in the eyes and said, "She doesn't know me. I love you. And I'm going to take care of my responsibility."

That gave me peace for a moment. But then the doubt crept in. How is this man going to take care of me and a baby? Then I remembered he had already been taking care of me. Buying me things and giving me money. He worked at a well-known university in our city, but then he quit. Yet, somehow, he never stopped providing. I didn't hit find out until later that he was a drug dealer. I didn't know anything about drugs, let alone how the game worked. But he had protected me so well, I wasn't afraid. I only knew one thing: I was pregnant, in high school, and still doing my best to maintain my grades.

He used to tell me, "For every A you bring home, I'll give you $100. For a B, $50."

So your girl brought home five A's and two B's.

He said, "I didn't know you were gonna have that many!"

Yes, I was a smart cookie. And he paid up.

The day after Christmas in 1990, the labor pains began. He never left my side. I was in labor for two days. Then, on December 28th, the most precious gift arrived, my firstborn. A bouncing baby boy, named after his father. He was overjoyed. After delivery, my mom pulled him aside. I thought maybe this was it. Maybe things were finally going to be alright. But after I'd healed and wanted to spend time with the family I had created, the same strictness returned.

Chapter Five
The Weight of Two Worlds

I wanted to bring my baby to his father's house, to spend time as a family. But the rules hadn't changed. I was still under her roof, still her responsibility. And in her eyes, I had already broken too many rules. She let me care for my son, but she guarded the boundaries like a warden. No visits. No overnights. No exceptions.

I felt trapped, like I was living in two worlds. In one, I was a mother, making bottles and singing lullabies. In the other, I was still a child, asking permission to breathe. I started sneaking out again, this time with a diaper bag instead of a backpack. She called the police AGAIN. He went to jail on the same charge! He bonded out. Nothing ever came of the charges. We fought even harder to be together. And yet, even in the rebellion, I felt the whisper again, "This isn't peace."

It wasn't condemnation. It wasn't shame. It was a gentle nudge, a reminder that I was made for more than sneaking and hiding. That love, real love, shouldn't have to be hidden in the shadows. But I didn't know how to get there. I didn't know how to bridge the gap between the girl my mother raised and the woman I was becoming. I only knew I was tired. Tired of pretending.

Tired of choosing between the two people I loved most my mother and my son's father.

One night, I sat on the edge of my bed, rocking my baby while the house slept. I whispered a prayer I hadn't said in a long time. "God, I don't know what I'm doing. But I need You. I need You to show me how to be a mother, how to be a daughter, how to be me." And for the first time in a long time, I felt a bit of peace. Not because everything was fixed. But because I had finally stopped running from Him, from myself, from the truth. I didn't have all the answers. But I had a baby in my arms, a prayer in my heart, and a God who still whispered to me in the dark.

As time went on, my mother finally got tired of fighting me.

One day, she looked at me and said, "You gon' see."

I wasn't moved. I thought I knew everything. So at seventeen, I packed up my things and moved in with my boyfriend. We got our first apartment.

I didn't go to prom. I didn't walk across the stage. But I did earn my high school diploma. And with that, I thought I had finally found freedom. Lo and behold, it was a sentence. Not behind bars but locked in my mind. Trapped in a world of highs and lows that I wasn't prepared for.

He was living his best life, making fast money by selling drugs, which he had mastered. He went from hustling on the corner to supplying the very dealers he once stood beside. Money was never an issue. If we needed it, we had it. If I wanted it, he got it. Sometimes, if I even looked at something too long, it would show up the next day, gift-wrapped in his affection. He was the true definition of a hustler. Our home was fully furnished. Bills paid. Fridge stocked. He took care of everything financially. But emotionally? I was running on empty. With more money came more options. And with more options came more women. Let the games begin.

The men he surrounded himself with were no better. Birds of a feather. They cheated on their girls, partied all night, and wore loyalty like a costume—something to take off when the lights went down. The clubbing. The late nights. The lies. THE PLAYER.

And there I was, pretty as a picture. Long, beautiful hair. Cute face, thin in the waist. Manicured nails. Dressed in the best. A beautiful baby boy on my hip. And still alone. I visited my family from time to time, but I mostly stayed around his. They knew what he was doing. No one dared say anything because he was that dude who didn't fear anyone or anything. I never told my family. I kept up the image. Every holiday, every gathering, we looked the part. Picture-perfect. He'd show up, smile, hold the baby (he was a good father), and kiss my cheek. Then, as soon as the food was eaten and the photos taken, he'd drop us off and disappear into the night. But my baby was my little best friend. He wasn't a fussy baby. He was calm, sweet, and full of light—my little Pooh Bear. I'd cuddle him close and feel a joy I couldn't explain. God knew I was going to need him, because in a world that was spinning out of control, he was my anchor. And even though I didn't know it yet, God was still writing my story—one whispered prayer, one sleepless night, one baby giggle at a time.

Chapter Six
When the Protector
Becomes the Pain

I kept a clean house. That was one thing I could control. No matter what chaos swirled outside, my home was spotless—my sanctuary. So when I came home one day and walked into the bedroom, something felt off. The only thing on the floor was a pair of his underwear. Just lying there. That was it. Nothing else was out of place. Just that. But something in my spirit stirred. Why is this the only thing on the floor? A woman's intuition is a powerful thing. I stood there, staring at that one piece of fabric as if it were a crime scene. And I knew somebody had been in my house.

I wasn't afraid of him. As bad as he was known to be in the streets, as much as his own family tiptoed around his temper, I never feared him. He had never given me a reason to.

So I asked. Boldly. "Who's been in my house? I know you didn't have a whore in here!"

He looked at me. And just like that, the truth came out. Because that's the kind of man he was, if you asked, he'd tell you. "Yes," he said. "There was someone here."

My heart dropped. Oh, this is what we're doing now?

"When I'm gone, you bring women into our home? Into the space I keep clean, where our baby sleeps?"

"No," he said. "This was the first time. I swear."

But the damage was done. The tears came fast. Hot. Heavy. The man I thought was my protector, the one who held me when I cried, who promised to take care of me, was now the one I needed protection from.

I collapsed onto the bed, sobbing. He came to console me and apologized.

As my sobbing continued, I said, "Daddy... why did you have to leave me?" Whispering it like a prayer. "I need you. Who's going to protect me now?" The grief I had buried came rushing back.

I wasn't just mourning betrayal; I was mourning the absence of the one man who had always made me feel safe."

God... why did You take my daddy away?" I didn't get an answer that night—just silence. But even in that silence, I felt something stir. Not comfort. Not peace. But a shift.

Because when the people you trust break you, and the ones you love can't protect you, you start looking for something deeper. Something eternal. Something holy. And though I didn't know it yet, that night was the beginning of my return. Not to him. But to the One who had never left.

Chapter Seven
Bound but Breaking Free

A lthough I was betrayed devastatingly, I didn't leave. He did what he always did, showered me with money, took me shopping, and wined and dined me until the sting dulled. And I stayed. But something in me had shifted.

I started going back to the church I'd grown up in since I was eight years old: Gethsemane Temple, COGIC. I couldn't stay away completely. The whisper of God's voice was always there, tugging at my spirit. Even in my rebellion, He never stopped calling me.

About a year later, my boyfriend was preparing for a major drug deal, one that could change everything. It did, but not like he planned. He never involved me in his business. I knew what he did, but he kept the details away from me. Still, my intuition kicked in hard that day.

"I wouldn't trust him," I told him.

He brushed me off. "You don't know nothing about the game. I went to school with this dude."

"Okay..." I said, but something didn't sit right.

That afternoon, I went to my best friend Nora's house and ended up spending the night. No calls. No check-ins. That wasn't like him. He never let me stay out without calling me. What is going on?

The next morning, I called his aunt's house. His cousin answered. "Hey, is he there?"

There was a pause. Then his cousin said, "He got busted yesterday. He's in jail." I froze.

"Stop playing. I'm serious, Toya," he said. "His bond is $250,000."

My heart pounded. Disbelief. Shock. And then... gratitude. God spared me. I told Nora. She barely blinked.

They were never close. She couldn't stand the way he treated me—and she definitely didn't understand why I stayed. I left her house and went straight to his family's. And just like that, he was already out. He made bail. And for a while, he acted right again.

Was it fear of prison? Or did he finally realize what he had in the family we'd built? Even in the middle of the mess, I kept popping up at church. That tug in my spirit wouldn't let go.

He stayed out on bond for over a year. Then came trial day. Guilty. He was facing 20 years. But by the grace of God, he was sentenced to five years in federal prison. My son and I traveled to Montgomery, Alabama, to visit him at the Air Force base where he was held. It didn't look or feel like a prison. But it was still a cage.

While he was locked up, I started to live—or at least I thought I was. I tried going to the club. But something strange kept happening. The music would be blasting, people dancing, and smoke in the air. And in the middle of it all, I'd start hearing praise songs in my ear.

Not the DJ. Not the speakers. Just in my spirit. Was I tripping? Did I catch a contact high from the weed smokers? I tried to drink those pretty little cocktails everyone else was sipping.

One sip, and my chest felt like it was on fire. Girl, this ain't for me. I'd leave the club at 5 AM and be at church by 8, singing in the choir like nothing happened. But something was happening. Something real. Then one day, something got a hold of me. It wasn't guilt. It wasn't fear.

It was the power of God. Right there in my mini skirt and big earrings, He met me. He was taking my life in a new direction. But I was still trying to drive down a dead-end road.

Chapter Eight
When Grace
Interrupts Chaos

He had wanted to marry me long before prison. I wasn't ready. But a year after I had my baby, I started planning the wedding. Yet something didn't feel right. So I stopped. Looking back, I realize I was moving off emotion, not prayer. And just because something seems right doesn't mean it's right for you. But eventually, I said yes. Not because I was sure. But because I didn't want to keep living any kind of way other than God's way while trying to walk with Him. So I married him while he was still in prison.

When he came home, I was hopeful. My husband. My family. My fresh start. He bought me a new car. Said the money came from what he'd saved before prison. But I knew better. He was selling drugs again, this time from the halfway house. That's all he knew.

At first, I was just happy to have him home. But it didn't take long for the cracks to show. I was becoming a woman of God. He was still committed to the gospel of the streets. We had outgrown each other. I had changed. He hadn't. He couldn't find a decent job, and at that time, he didn't want to let go of the streets. The fun times were few. The tension was constant. I guess He didn't like the woman I was becoming, stronger, wiser, more rooted in God.

While he was locked up, I had grown. His best friend helped pay my bills for a while, but I still worked. I took care of myself. I came into my own. And my relationship with God deepened. But our marriage? It became a distraction—two people, thinking and heading in two different directions. I didn't want to choose. So God let the choice be made for me.

He met her at a McDonald's drive-thru. Came home with our food and said,

This chick tried to holler at me through the window. Gave me her number. I tore it up, though—she wasn't my type."

Oh really? Lo and behold, that same woman ended our ten-year relationship. I was devastated. I had waited for him and visited him. Prayed for him. And this is what I got?

She got pregnant almost immediately. And he brought her around his family as if I didn't exist. I lost it. She knew about me. She knew he was married. And still, she pursued him. I confronted her at his grandparents' house. I punched her in the face. A fight broke out. He grabbed me, trying to hold me back.

"Please stop," he begged.

"You're holding me?" I screamed.

"You caused this! "She grabbed a Corona bottle to hit me in the head.

Oh really? I broke loose and started throwing everything I could get my hands on—spoons, the toaster, whatever was within reach. I was uncontrollable. I started fighting him, too. It was chaos. They left.

She called the police. A warrant was issued for my arrest. But God stepped in. My pastor, who also served as the head chaplain at the jail, called and had me released before I even arrived. When the DA heard the whole story, the case was thrown out.

She knew he was married. She knew of me. She had heard how well he took care of me. I guess she wanted a piece of the pie. But I had no choice but to let it go. I didn't understand the pain. I didn't understand the betrayal. I remember sitting at home, crying. My Pooh Bear, just five years old, was the only one who could comfort me. God used that baby to hold me together. I couldn't function for six months. I went to church, but I was just there. Going through the motions. But even in my brokenness, God was with me. That whisper never left.

I remember praying, "God, if You take this pain away, I will never put myself in this situation again." One day, I was driving with

Pooh Bear in the back seat. And I heard it—loud and clear.

"Everything is going to be alright." I turned around.

"Pooh Bear, did you hear that?"

He said, "Yes."

That moment changed everything. My pastor's wife took me under her wing. She nurtured me. Taught me. Tough-loved me back to life. And slowly, I shook it off. The pain. The shame. The weight of a marriage that was never meant to be. My relationship with God blossomed. I wasn't just around church anymore. I was in it—for real.

Chapter Nine
Unlocked but Unfinished

A tlanta wasn't part of my plan. But when my cousin Becky moved there and said, "Come see if you like it," something in me said, Why not?

My pastor's wife supported the temporary move, and my Pooh Bear stayed behind with his father and her. I locked up my house, packed my bags, and set out for the unknown.

It was my first time in Atlanta, and Becky made me feel right at home. She was a natural prankster, always up to something. Her laughter was wild and contagious, and for the first time in a long time, I found myself laughing too.

One day, she said, "Tez, I have someone I want you to meet."

I shut that down quickly. "Nope."

But she kept pushing: "Just a friendship, nothing else."

She painted the picture: tall, brown-skinned, fresh haircut, drives a new Diamante. I still wasn't sold. But Becky was relentless. Finally, I agreed on a date, just a meet-and-greet at her place.

"He'll be here at 7 PM," she said.

Then, about fifteen minutes before he arrived, Becky came to me with that mischievous smirk.

"Tez, I have something to tell you."

I braced myself.

"He's really short, one of his eyes randomly leaks water, and he's musty all the time." Then she laughed uncontrollably.

That was it, I burst out laughing and had to shut myself in the room. NO THANK YOU.

Still, my time in Atlanta was beautiful. I made new friends, even dated a guy for a while, but it didn't go anywhere. I realized I needed to focus on myself and my Pooh Bear. So I returned to New Orleans. Home was just as I left it, quiet, familiar, waiting.

I enrolled in school. Though I had my own home, my pastor's wife insisted I stay with them. She even asked my mother for permission—mind you, I was grown!

Every morning at 5 AM, my pastor would cook breakfast and call out, "Daughter, come get your breakfast before it gets cold."

It reminded me of my father. He used to do the same. I felt safe. I felt seen. I felt...loved.

Two years passed. I was single, free, and finally smiling for real. I worked weekends at my mom's 24-hour sitting service and stayed focused on school. I wanted more out of life. I was hungry for it. Freedom felt like fresh air—and forgiveness was the oxygen.

I watched my mother and my pastor's wife—two strong women who worked hard and never made excuses.

One day, my pastor's wife told me, "If you get your education, a man can never take that from you. You'll always be able to take care of yourself."

That stuck with me. Not to throw accomplishments in a man's face, but to always have a plan B. Just in case.

After graduation, I landed a job at a doctor's office with a salary that made me proud. I bought a new car—on my own. I was doing the thing. INDEPENDENTLY. God is so good. Life was good. My son, Frederick (Pooh Bear), and I were thriving.

Then came the call. It was my cousin on my daddy's side. She and her husband had started a ministry and were hosting a special service with a guest preacher. She invited me to come. I wanted to support her, so I went. And just like that...here I go again.

Chapter Ten
The Preacher, the Mask, and the Mirror

I arrived at their church, not expecting much, just there to support my cousin and her husband's new ministry. The service was good. The guest preacher got up—he was a prophet. And not just any prophet, he could sing, preach, and prophesy with such power that the whole room leaned in. Then he called me out. He gave me a prophetic word that hit every mark. I was stunned. But one thing puzzled me: he said he saw me writing children's books. I didn't know what to make of that. Twenty years later, I'd come to understand it fully. But in that moment, I tucked it away in my heart.

After service, my cousin and her husband introduced me to him. Here they go, matchmaking on the slick. We all went out to dinner. Let the shenanigans begin. We started dating. He was mild-mannered, very nice. Fourteen years older than me, but he didn't look it. Nice build, wore glasses. Said he was a father of four, married twice before. We talked, prayed, and built a friendship. He gave me his whole paycheck every pay period. Came to my house and left. No living together, no sexual encounters, very few kisses. Could this be the real thing?

Then one night, we were sitting on my bed. He was at the foot, and I was at the head, diagonally across from each other. In the middle of his talking, I saw it—a mask. An evil mask flashed across his face quickly, like someone putting it on and snatching it off. I rubbed my eyes. He kept talking.

Then it happened again. Okay, God... what is this? I didn't say a word. I let him go home.

Time passed. He wanted to marry me. I was skeptical. We went to another church service together, and we both got called out.

The woman said, "You don't want to marry him, and you're giving him a hard time. He's your husband."

I said to myself, Excuse me? Ma'am, you don't know me or him. What is this? My friend Janice was with us. We both looked at each other like, Ruh-roh (in my best Scooby-Doo voice). Still, a small wedding was planned.

The day came. I was sitting in the car, dressed and ready, but my spirit wasn't. My mom's friend—who called me her daughter—was sitting with me.

I turned to her and said, "I changed my mind. I don't want to do this."

She said, "You're just nervous. Cold feet."

"No, I'm not. I don't want to get married."

"You can't do this. His family is here. Your family is here. How is that going to look?"

I said, "I don't care about none of that. My family will turn this into a party." But she kept talking. And I gave in.

I got out of the car. Went in. Got married. Everything seemed fine. I left the church I grew up in—my pastor and his wife understood. I had to follow my husband. We joined a five-fold ministry, and I grew a lot under that teaching. But thirty days in... the mask I saw that night revealed itself. He wanted to control me. THE PREACHER??? Wait—what? Where do they do that at? Not this chic!

I was still working at the doctor's office. He told me I was supposed to give him my checkbook and let him control the money. Excuse me? Oh, and that whole "Here's my paycheck" thing? Out the window. The same window I wanted to throw him out of.

He had moved into my house because I wasn't about to uproot myself. I politely asked him to leave my house.

He stood in the doorway of my bedroom and said, "We've been married 30 days. You're stuck with me."

I said, "Oh yeah? Imma show you. 'Hello, 911.'"

He left immediately. Don't play with me. My niece Shawneice, my Ne-Ne, and my Pooh Bear witnessed it all. I hated that they had to see it, but thank God, it didn't affect them. I was done. I remembered the promise I made to God: If You heal my heart from that first relationship, I won't put myself in a position to cry over a man again. And I didn't. A few days later, my phone rang...Who could that be?

Chapter Eleven
Here I Go Again

T he phone rang. It was the preacher.

I'm sorry," he said. "Please forgive me."
Me?

"Forgiven," I told him, "I'll see you at church tomorrow."

We were back at church. The service was good. I was told to give him a chance. Now that he knows I ain't the one, maybe he'll act right. Boom, he came home.

We talked. He said, "I'm going to take the first paycheck and pay all the bills, get that out of the way so you don't have to worry about anything." Sounded good, right? Just wait. I was being a wife—cooking, cleaning, working, taking care of my Pooh Bear and Ne-Ne. Just being me. Loving, caring, nurturing. Never fussy. I don't like to argue. I've always smiled and loved to laugh. Praying and loving God with my whole heart. I had a real relationship with Him, personal, intimate, unshakable. But something wasn't right. His wallet would sit on the dresser Monday through Thursday. But on payday Fridays? It disappeared. I noticed he started putting it on the shelf in the closet. I could've gone in and gotten it if I wanted to. But I didn't.

I asked politely, "What are we paying today?"

He said, "Oh, I didn't have any plans on paying anything today."

I said, "Okay." But inside? I was boiling. You think I'm going to pay these bills myself while you live here for free and get between these legs? Okay.

I paid the bills because I didn't want to fall behind. I didn't tell him. He didn't ask. I kept doing my duties as a wife, taking care of my babies. Never mistreated him. I stayed focused. The following week came. I asked again. Same response. But this time, he came home with the latest cell phone, pretty blue, I might add. Oh yeah? I went for a drive. I love talking to God in my car.

As I drove, I said, "God, I'm trying with everything in me to make this marriage work. But if yo' boy don't pay no bills next week, that's strike three. He's outta there."

I went back home and kept being my normal self. No arguments. The house was quiet. Then came payday. And would you believe it? The preacher told me the same thing again.

I said, "The Bible says, 'But if any provide not for his own, and especially for those of his own house, he hath denied the faith, and is worse than an infidel.'" (1 Timothy 5:8)

He knew the Word like the back of his hand. But he wasn't practicing what he preached. He asked me to take him to work. By now, I was like Popeye:

"That's all I can stands, and I can't stands no more!"

I told him, "No."

We exchanged words. He told me I was "about a D and a dollar." I had to laugh. Really? He kept talking, provoking me. Got in my face. Later, I found out he used to fight his women. Not me. Before I knew it, I snatched his eyeglasses off his face and broke them in half. Snatched his pager off his hip and slammed it on the floor. Broke that brand-new phone he bought—with the bill money. Then out came my babies. Ne-Ne stood on his left. Pooh Bear on his right.

Ne-Ne said, "You better not touch my auntie."

Pooh Bear, in his deep voice, said, "If you touch my momma, I will hurt you."

I don't know if he thought he was going to beat me that day, but he saw I wasn't afraid. I guess he rethought that thing.

I called my momma. She came over, looked at me, and said, "Tez, you're pregnant."

Girl, what? I told her, "I can't have any more children."

She said, "Alright. I don't care what you say. You gon' see." (Annie Mae's favorite words when she knows she's right. LOL.)

The preacher left with my mother. The kids made sure I was okay. We went to bed. I got an appointment with the doctor. And I was pregnant. Oh nooooooo. Tears fell. Here I go again.

Chapter Twelve
The Preacher's Final Altar

T welve years later... and I was having another baby. I didn't know what to do. I went to church, and after the service, I broke down crying.

My first lady came over and asked, "What are you crying for?"

I said, "I don't want my baby to look like him."

She looked me square in the face and said boldly, "Stop crying. God ain't gon' do that to you."

I immediately stopped crying and started laughing. I had never heard anything like that before. I mean—it's DNA, right?... But God. Let's just say he looks just like me. Yes, I had another baby boy. He was precious—a gift. I named him Destin. I always allowed him to visit with his son. And according to his mother, he began to brag about Destin.

She told me, "This is the only child he's come home and talked about. I can't wait to meet him."

Destin went to meet his grandparents. They loved him. They received him. But a few months later, his skin changed. He started having issues. A severe case of eczema, and unable to tolerate formula. Over 100 allergies. We were in and out of the hospital. And I was doing it alone.

I enrolled in nursing school. I had to make a move. At the time, getting into a nursing program was tough—waiting lists everywhere. But God opened a door. I took the entrance exam, passed the first time, and got a call for the next class. I couldn't miss this life-changing opportunity. But Destin couldn't go to daycare. His condition was too risky. I didn't know what I was going to do. Then one Sunday after church, a kind soul—someone I trusted—came to me and said, "I will keep your baby." I knew right then God was in the plan.

Later, my mom stepped in to help. The preacher would come to see Destin, buy him things from time to time. But we never got back together. No animosity. No bitterness. He tried to rekindle things, but I declined. I was in nursing school. I needed no distractions.

God was taking care of me. One night, I had a dream. I saw him in an open green field, crying. The next day, he called. I told him about the dream. He said, "My crying days are over."

I simply said, "Okay."

Destin was turning one. I booked a birthday party for him at Chuck E. Cheese. The preacher asked what to buy him. I said, "A Power Wheels car."

He said, "Okay."

I said, "Thank you."

Then he said, "I love you."

I said, "I love you, too."

I wondered why he said those three words to me. I didn't know that would be our last conversation.

About two hours after I arrived at school, I heard my name called over the intercom. "Rutez Mason, please come to the office." My heart dropped. Something's wrong with my baby. I ran. The office was a good distance from my classroom, but I didn't care. I was out of breath, bent over, trying to catch my breath when I got there. It was my sister.

She must've seen the panic in my eyes because the first thing she said was, "Destin is fine." I exhaled. Smiled.

Then she said, "They found the preacher dead... in the trunk of his car."

Oh no! Three days before Destin's first birthday. My heart sank. My mind raced. God, where is his soul? Did he make it right with You? He preached, prophesied, prayed for others... but did he come out of the pit he was in? No one knew my thoughts but God. And God, being God, sent someone to me.

They said, "He didn't die instantly. He had a little talk with Jesus. And God allowed him to make it in."

My heart was relieved. Because I care about souls. Then came the funeral planning. My church family was a blessing. But guess what? While we were married, he had a mistress. She used to be in the services where he ministered. She had a baby girl for him—one none of us knew about. Not me. Not his family. The baby was born six months after Destin. He never acknowledged her.

Days before the funeral, I got a call. "Hello, Tez. This Blackie." (Not her real name.)

She said, "Can me and the baby come to the funeral?"

"No ma'am, you cannot. You have the nerve to call me now? You were sleeping with my husband and kept quiet. He never signed your baby's birth certificate. Never acknowledged her. All you have is a wet tail and memories. If he slept with you, who else was he with?

That's probably why he didn't claim the child. It's sad you dragged a baby into your mess. Have a nice life." Click.

The day came to lay him to rest. So much was going on—women, people, babies. My church arranged for security. Destin sat in the choir stand with his godparents. They understood the assignment: Let no one touch him. The service was lively. Singing. Praising. Shouting. Bishop Worthy preached a powerful eulogy. Then came the viewing. Here comes the first wife—in a leather suit. In July. I knew then...

He was an Army veteran, so he was buried at the Veterans Cemetery. They honored him and presented me with the flag. The first wife tried it. She lingered by the casket after everyone else had moved. I saw her talking to a General.

A relative came to me and said, "She told that man she's the wife and she's getting your paperwork."

Oh really? I walked over, calm and collected.

"Hi," I said to the General.

He asked, "Who are you?"

"I'm Rutez Moore. The wife of the deceased."

He pulled back what he was about to hand her and placed it in the rightful hands—mine. I gave her a look like, Girl, you need to get back.

She asked, "Can I get a flower?"

I said, "You can take the whole casket spray if you want to. Just doing too much. Girl, y'all been divorced."

The preacher was laid to rest. And I had to move on. They never found out who the murderer was or exactly what happened. I had two sons and Ne-Ne to raise and nursing school.

I looked in the mirror and said, "Tez, you got this." And I heard God whisper back, I got you.

Chapter Thirteen
God Didn't Just Speak— He Covered

I graduated from nursing school and passed my board exam on the first try. That alone was a testimony. I landed my first job as a nurse and stepped into a new season— single, free, and focused. No dating. No man. Just church, work, and my babies. I had a long-distance friend in California who would text every now and then to check in, but that was it. I was content. Life was peaceful.

Then came 2005. Hurricane Katrina. We evacuated. And I didn't return to New Orleans. Born and raised in that city, and it literally washed away. It was heartbreaking. But I thank God for my nursing license. It made it easier to transition. My kids were young, so to them, it felt like a road trip. They were living their best lives, unaware of the storm we had just escaped. We had everything we needed and more. Thanks to God. We relocated to Texas.

Later, my sister and I traveled back to New Orleans when the city reopened, just to assess the damage. On our way back to Texas, we saw a sign: Donaldsonville.

My sister said, "Didn't Ree evacuate here? Call and see if she's around."

Now Ree—my mama's friend, who we looked at like a second mother—was the same woman who sat in the car with me the day I tried not to marry the preacher—the same one who talked me into going through with it. I called. She answered.

"Come on," she said. "I'll be glad to see y'all." She gave us the address. We pulled up.

She was temporarily staying with her cousin— she had lost everything in Katrina, too. I guess he was checking me out. I probably was checking him out too... maybe. I was too busy eating that fried fish and good ol' potato salad to be sure. We stayed for about an hour or so.

Laughed. Talked. Then we left. That was all. Or so I thought. Who knew that taking this detour on the way back to Texas......would almost lead me to a dead end. LITERALLY.

Ree got settled in Donaldsonville and said, "Come down here."

Not thinking much of it, I did go, just to visit. Ree and I had always been close, especially since I'd been single for so long. We hung out, laughed, and caught up like old times.

Then here she goes: "Girl, somebody sweet on you." I said, "Who?" She pointed to her cousin.

"Every time he comes over here, he picks up this picture of you and says, 'I'm going to get with her.'" I laughed.

"Don't be trying to hook me up with him just because he's your cousin."

She said, "He's a good man. Divorced."
"Why?" I asked.

She told me his ex-wife cheated on him—had the man in his house while he was at work and ended up pregnant. That broke him. Oh wow, I thought. Okay. I'll see. He invited me to his job's Christmas party. I represented well, I might add. He was nice and fun to be around. We had good conversations, went to balls, and just enjoyed each other's company.

Time passed, and I moved from Texas to Donaldsonville. I said, "This is it," but deep down, I wasn't sure. I just knew I'd be near Ree, and I wanted to see where this would go.

I'd been single for a long time. He had one son who lived with him. We'd hang out with the boys. But Pooh Bear— almost 16 at the time— wasn't feeling it. He and Ne-Ne went to stay with my mom. They were Annie Mae's favorites, so she welcomed them with open arms. I provided financially and visited often. It was only an hour's drive. I worked in New Orleans while living in Donaldsonville.

After dating for a while, he proposed. I accepted. Ree was thrilled. Pooh Bear...not so much. He never said why. The man treated them like his own. He was clean, kept a tidy house, cooked well, and loved God. I figured maybe Pooh Bear just wanted me to stay single—he saw I was doing well on my own. I started planning a big wedding. I'd never had a real one before, and I told myself, I'm going big this time. This is it.

He was thoughtful, romantic, and a family man. Everyone in his circle said he was a good person— and I saw it too. Then one day, I walked into his house and saw a book on the table. The title was something like *Why Do Men Turn Gay?* I can't remember exactly. Then I went to the computer and saw a dating site pulled up with men.

So, me being me, I asked.

He said, "That's my nephew." I closed the computer. He removed the book. His nephew was around often and seemed a little extra but not flat-out obvious. Was this my sign? Did I ignore it? He didn't act that way. Nothing extra. So I kept planning the wedding. The day came. We had a beautiful wedding. We were happy. Living our best life, no arguing. He cooked. I helped clean—especially the bathroom, because I like mine sterilized. I'd work, come home, shower, and relax. He was thoughtful—a true family man.

I was pregnant. But my baby girl died in my womb. They tested me for everything. There was no explanation for her death. I remember the doctor walking in and saying, "All your tests were negative—including HIV."

I looked at him and said, "And that's how I want to stay." It just came out of my mouth.

He said, "You don't have to worry about that."

That was the most devastating time in my life. I finally got my baby girl—and she didn't make it. I delivered a stillborn. She was the prettiest thing I'd ever seen. Nothing looked wrong. She even had gray eyes. We held a graveside service and buried her in his family plot. Seven months later, I was pregnant again. Fertile Myrtle. This baby kicked my butt. I was in my late 30s—high risk. I had to take a baby aspirin every day until delivery. I saw the fetal maternal medicine doctor and my OB twice a month.

Finally, I went into labor. They called in the whole pediatric team. They thought the baby would be in respiratory distress. But he came out healthy as could be. BUT GOD. God told me to name him Elijah. My husband was a good father. He took care of me during postpartum. We had a good friendship. He worked, came home, and stayed home with his family.

Six weeks passed. We went to his church. He introduced me to a guy who kept asking him to join the choir. He hesitated. I didn't know why at the time. Maybe he knew. Maybe he knew that would be his downfall. I'm saying it's just a choir. Maybe to him, it wasn't just a choir. It was who was in the choir. He gave it some thought. Then he joined. And the tambourine played...

After he joined the choir, I noticed a change. He stopped calling me on his way to work. We stopped praying together. The intimacy faded. The connection dimmed. But I didn't say anything, just watched. He never came home late. The only time he was away was on Sundays when I was away. I stayed at my church in New Orleans and visited his occasionally. Something was off.

One day, he came home, and as always, I greeted him with joy. "Hey," I said.

He smiled. "Hey, bae."

But something didn't sit right. His eyes were red. He looked...different. I leaned in to hug him. He worked for the post office, and it was a hot, sunny day. But when my nose brushed his neck, I smelled Dove soap. We didn't have Dove soap in the house. Hmm. I didn't say anything.

But my thoughts were racing. He went to shower—his usual routine. Maybe to throw me off. But little did he know, the covers were being pulled back.

Then strange things started happening. Every time I walked out of my front door, I'd hear a whisper: Look to the left. And there he was. A strange man. Same car. Just sitting there. Watching. I kept living my life. But my husband's life was shifting—his true desires surfacing.

A few days later, I looked at him and said, "Something's not right with you. You're acting different."

He told me his blood pressure was up, and he had gone to see his doctor. Then he said, "I got something to tell you."

"Okay."

"Back in the day, when I was a correctional officer, an inmate with HIV bit me. I have to be tested."

Wait, what? Why do you need to be tested now? I've had two babies. No HIV. This doesn't sound right.

I went to a revival at my church. The bishop from Mobile, Alabama, called me out first. He said, "I'm just going to tell you straight— HE'S GAY. It's the men in the choir."

He said two of them had plotted to kill me— but the fear of God stopped them. That explains the man in the car. I stood there, stunned. My family was in the room. I was humiliated. Confused. Angry.

Then the bishop said, "And nobody in here better not repeat anything I told her to anyone."

I went home that night and asked for his phone. He gave it to me. Everything was in there. The phone I bought him. The messages. The voicemails. The lies. The way he made it seem like I was the one blocking him from being with them. I gasped for air.

"You like boys??? Why did you pursue me? Was I your cover-up?"

Then came the final blow: he tested positive for HIV. I was no good. Not ashamed—just broken. I've always been a protector. If I had told my brothers or Pooh Bear, they would've destroyed him. I loved them too much to put blood on their hands. But I wanted him dead. He had put a possible death sentence on me. He got cocky. Cold. He didn't care anymore.

I fell on my face and cried out to God. I travailed like never before. "God, I repent. I need You to hear my cry today. Don't let me die this way. I don't deserve this. My boys need me. Please, God..."

Then the whisper cut me off: Don't say that you don't want to be married again. He had something greater in store. Then the whisper said: Read John 14:14.

I wasn't a Bible scholar then, nor was I reading my Bible at the time. Oh, but did I start reading the chapters daily! God had my undivided attention. I opened my Bible to that scripture. It said, "If ye shall ask anything in my name, I will do it."

I cried uncontrollably. God answered me immediately. Despite my shortcomings. Despite not getting it right every time. In the midst of this, my sister Jean, who was my best friend, had passed. But joy came, Pooh Bear's daughter, Markenzi, was born! She was perfect. Looked just like me.

He was referred to an infectious disease doctor, Dr. G. He told her the same lie about the inmate. Told her about me. Her clinic was closed on Fridays. But she opened it—just for me. She sat me down and explained HIV. How it works. How it's transmitted.

She said, "Don't leave your husband. It's not his fault."

Then I pulled out the phone. Let her hear the voicemails.

She looked at me and said, "That liar."

Then she said the words that echoed in my soul: "God is not going to do this to you."

I left her office and went to the lab. Got my blood drawn and waited.

Seven days. The longest seven days of my life. I couldn't eat. Couldn't sleep. Couldn't focus. Just kept asking, Who's going to raise my boys? Planning my funeral in my head. Is this the end? Still hearing the whisper: I got you. Tears...

It was time to see Dr. G. I walked into her office, and the weight of it all hit me. Everyone in that waiting room knew why I was there. It made me sick to my stomach that this man had done this to me. They called me back. I was placed in a room. Then I heard her voice down the hall:

"Where is she? I have to get to her."

Somehow, I knew she was talking about me. She burst into the room and said boldly, "You don't have it!"

Dr. G and I went into full praise. We hugged.

We cried. She was so happy for me. Then she said, "You have to come back in 30 days." What? "That's how it goes," she said. Okay.

During that time, my prayer life deepened. My Word life grew. The whisper became a voice. God gave me strength. Thirty days later, I went back to the lab. Then back to her office. Again, I heard her voice: "Where is she?"

She came in and said it again: "You don't have it!" We praised again.

"Come back in six months," she said.

Six months passed. I returned.

"You don't have it," she said. Then she looked me in the eye and said, "The only way you'll get it is if you go out there yourself.

You don't have to worry about that, suga!

I called him. "I don't have it," I said.

His response? Cold. Distant.

I said, "You wanted me to have it? Are you crazy?"

He said, "That's not it."

"Then what is it?"

We hung up. I guess he called his little crew to tell them. I said to myself, He needs to pay for what he did to me. He has no remorse. I'm going to show him. Then the voice of God said clearly: "Vengeance is mine, and I will repay."

I snapped back: "What do you mean, vengeance is Yours? Do you know what he did to me?" As if God didn't already know. As if He hadn't seen it all.

Then He said, "Did I let you die?" I broke. I bawled my eyes out. God wanted my heart free. I'd be lying if I said I forgave him right away. It took time. And the more I prayed and studied, the cockier he got. He even asked me to leave. I was already planning to go, but I was trying to figure it out. It got so bad that I left abruptly. Moved in with Ree for a month or so. Then I got my own house in New Orleans. Had to buy all new furniture. I was in hustle mode. But God kept me. He kept my mind. Still, New Orleans wasn't the same. I needed more. My kids needed better opportunities. So I moved to Texas. Landed a job. And became the Director of Health & Wellness. God blessed me.

Chapter Fourteen
BUT GOD...

Texas wasn't just a relocation—it was a resurrection. After everything I'd been through, I needed a fresh start. A new place to breathe. A place where my children could thrive and I could finally exhale. God opened the door.

I landed a job, and not just any job—I became the Director of Health & Wellness. The same girl who once cried out on her face, begging God not to let her die, was now leading others in healing and wellness. Being a Director of Nursing gave me the opportunity to pay forward what God has done for me. Only God. I walked into that role with authority, compassion, and a quiet strength that had been forged in fire. I wasn't just a nurse—I was a woman who had survived betrayal, heartbreak, and near-death despair. I was a mother, a provider, a protector, and a prayer warrior. I was whole. God forgave me loud, so

I forgave others gently—and that became my power.

My children were growing. Elijah was a big boy now, Destin was thriving, and no more sickness! Pooh Bear and Ne-Ne were finding their own paths. And me? I was finally learning how to live again, not just survive. I wasn't bitter anymore. I was better. I found joy in the little things—morning prayer, gospel music in the car, laughter with my kids, quiet moments with God. I didn't need a man to complete me. I was already full. But I wasn't closed off either. I knew that if God had someone for me, it would be in His time, not mine. I wasn't chasing love. I was walking in purpose. And purpose was enough. I began mentoring others—young nurses, single mothers, women who had been through what I had.

My story wasn't just mine anymore. It was a lifeline for someone else. I started writing again. The whisper I once heard became a calling. My first Children's book. Healing through storytelling. Ministering God'sWord. God was using every broken piece of my past to build something beautiful. And then—God did something I didn't expect.

I'm a nurse. I've been in healthcare. But this next chapter wasn't about my career—it was about covenant. My longtime friend from California—the son of my first pastor and first lady, the ones who took me under their wings—had moved back to New Orleans to care for his parents. He was single and free. So was I.

His father was turning 90, and they were planning a big celebration. I called his mom to check in, and she said, "Call Brad to get your ticket. I did.

He answered on half a ring and said, "What do I owe this pleasure?"

I laughed. "Man, I need a ticket to your daddy's birthday celebration. You buying it?"

Long story short—he did. We kept talking. I already knew him. He was genuinely kind and thoughtful. Loving. Nothing was too good for me. He showed me what a true man of God was made of. He was an ordained Elder, had taught school for 23 years, and loved God deeply. Just like his father—a man of integrity, a man after God's own heart. I said, Lissen, God... I can't take anymore. What do You say about this? And for the first time, I truly acknowledged God in all my ways. His approval was upon it. We married. He has never changed in all these years.

I love me some him! My true soul mate. My kids love him, and he loves them. Fast forward. And now—he's the pastor, and I'm the first lady of the very church I grew up in. Returned, Restored, Recommissioned.

God routed me back to my humble beginnings. It was preordained from the beginning of time. He allowed me to make mistakes. To learn. To grow. To realize that I couldn't do it on my own. But He never left me.

The voice didn't shout. It never boomed or thundered like I sometimes imagined God might. It was gentle, almost like a breeze brushing past my ear when everything else around me was storming. That voice found me in empty rooms, in crowded kitchens, in the quiet moments when I tried to make sense of why life hurt so much. It didn't always give answers. But it gave me peace.

Even as a little girl, I understood that the voice was different from my own thoughts. It brought calm when I was anxious, strength when I felt broken, and hope when there didn't seem to be any. It was like being wrapped in an invisible hug when I felt like no one in the world could see me.

Sometimes, I'd be on the floor of my room, tears soaking the carpet, and I'd hear: "You're stronger than you know." Other times, when I felt unloved or unwanted, it would come gently: "You are mine. I have not forgotten you." That voice became my lifeline.

Over time, I started talking back—not out loud, but in my heart. I would whisper "thank yous" when I made it through a hard day. I'd ask for guidance when I didn't know who to trust. And slowly, the whisper began to feel like a relationship. Not a religion, not a rulebook—but a God who was personal, present, and patient.

Faith didn't happen overnight. It built itself layer by layer, like bricks in a wall I didn't know I was building—one that would hold me up when I couldn't hold myself.

Forgiveness was the mortar between those bricks.

I had to forgive the ones who wounded me, the ones who left me, and even the version of myself that didn't know her worth. Forgiveness didn't come easily. It came through tears, through prayer, through surrender. But it was the key to my healing.

It was through my pain that my prayer life developed. My ministry was birthed in the fire of affliction. I don't just speak under God's anointing—I minister from a place of freedom. I am healed. Delivered. Whole.

God hurt me out of some things. Yes, it hurt. But it healed. It didn't always feel good, but it pushed me into destiny. The blessings of Abraham rest on me. I'm not just called—I'm chosen. I know my worth, and God allows me to teach others theirs.

He gave me beauty for ashes. He collected every tear. My eyes are dry now, and my vision is clear. I'm focused. I'm favored. God heard me—and He answered.

There were still hard days. There were still moments when the tears came uninvited. But I wasn't alone anymore. The little girl who used to sit in silence with no one to talk to had found a friend who never left. A protector who didn't need a cape. A Father who wasn't gone.

I began to see life through a different lens—not just as something I had to endure, but something I was being prepared for. That still small voice? It created a warrior.

Meet the Author
Rutez Mason

Rutez Mason, a native of New Orleans, now resides in Keller, TX, and walks boldly in her divine calling as Director of Health & Wellness, First Lady, mentor, and minister. She is the prophetic voice behind *I AM LOVED,* her first children's book. Founder of Jazzy Tazzy Kids, Rutez nurtures generations. Mother to Frederick, Destin, Elijah; bonus mom to Tywon; godmother to Joseph and Rodd; "grandtee" to Chris'Siana, Christopher, Christian, Case'Yiana; and grandmother to Markenzi. Alongside her husband, Pastor Bradford LeViege, she ministers healing, hope, and restoration.